THE A TO Z OF GRAND PRIX

Written by **Charlotte Morgan**

This edition first published in the UK in 2009
By Green Umbrella Publishing

© Green Umbrella Publishing 2009

www.gupublishing.co.uk

Publishers Jules Gammond and Vanessa Gardner

Printed and bound in Italy

ISBN: 978-1-906635-26-8

The views in this book are those of the author but they are general views
only and readers are urged to consult the relevant and qualified specialist for
individual advice in particular situations.

Contents

Introduction

Formula One, "F1" racing is one of the most exciting, and expensive, sports in the world. Governed by the Fédération Internationale de l'Automobile (FIA), the stakes are high for drivers, constructors and sponsors alike and the economic effect of the sport across the globe is significant. Divided into two world championships (for drivers and constructors), Grands Prix are usually held on purpose-built circuits, however, some races are run over closed public roads.

The Grand Prix de Pau in 1901 was the first race to be given a name that is synonymous with motor racing the world over today. But the name wasn't in general usage until the Automobile Club de France (ACF) adopted it as its own five years later.

On 26 June 1906, the ACF organised an event near Le Mans in France with a starting field of 32 cars, which raced over a 65 mile (105 kilometre) triangular course. Split over two days, there were just 11 cars remaining in the race by the time the drivers reached lap 12. Despite the fact that it usually took around 15 minutes to change tyres on racing cars, Michelin led the way by ingeniously creating detachable rims,

▲ Singapore; the latest circuit to join the Grand Prix.

◀ The 1906 Automobile Grand Prix.

enabling the tyres on Ferenc Szisz's car to be removed and new ones added in a staggering two to three minutes. Hungarian Szisz won the race in his 90hp Renault, having been able to save valuable time in the pit.

From this point on, the Grand Prix in Le Mans signalled the start of an era, and the sport celebrated its centenary in 2006. But, racing was heavily nationalistic and many countries had different rules while most races were run over closed public roads rather than purpose-built tracks. By the early 1920s, however, various countries were beginning to run a collection of races with similar rules and, in 1924, various national motor clubs formed the Association Internationale des Automobile Clubs Reconnus (AIACR) of which the Commission Sportive Internationale (CSI) began regulating international racing and ultimately the Grand Prix before the days of the FIA.

The centre for Grand Prix racing has remained firmly in Europe throughout its development, although these massive television events attracting millions of viewers and spectators, are held worldwide. In 1999, new circuits were added in Bahrain, China, Malaysia, Turkey and the US. The race is developing constantly and, in 2008, Singapore held the sport's first night race while India is set to join the Grand Prix circuit in 2010.

Alesi

Always popular with the *tifosi* (Italian supporters), Giovanni "Jean" Alesi made his racing debut in the 1989 French Grand Prix where he showed his potential by finishing fourth. Alesi (born on 11 June 1964 in Avignon, Sicily) found his form the following year driving for Tyrrell in what were widely considered under-performing vehicles compared to the likes of Williams and Ferrari. Despite this, he managed to lead for 25 laps in his first US Grand Prix in Phoenix – in front of Ayrton Senna – and eventually claimed second place. He followed this with another runner's-up spot in Monaco and, by 1991, all the top teams wanted Alesi to drive for them.

Although not particularly renowned for being sensational, he went on to enjoy one of the longest careers in motor racing. He celebrated having reached his 200th race in 2001 and had enjoyed standing on the podium 32 times. However, he only gained one victory; he had an emotional win on his 31st birthday in Montreal at the 1995 Canadian Grand Prix.

Alesi's career saw spells with Benetton, Sauber, Prost, Jordan and Ferrari as well as Tyrrell. He ended his F1 days in 2001 and after retiring from DTM (German Touring Car Championship) driving in 2006 now spends his time at his vineyard in Sicily.

◀◀ Jean Alesi
in 1994.

◀ Jean Alesi
winning the 1995
Canadian Grand
Prix.

Alonso

Born in Oviedo, northern Spain on 29
July 1981, Fernando Alonso Diaz, won
the world drivers' championship on 25
September 2005 at the tender age of 24;
making him the youngest F1 champion.
Nicknamed "El Nano", he then became
the second driver – after Michael
Schumacher – to score at least 100

points for three consecutive seasons.

His career began in karts where his
skill and determination soon earned
him the sponsorship required to begin
fulfilling his dream of becoming a full-
time F1 driver. He had his first test in
a racing car in October 1998 at the
Albacete Circuit where, as a result of lap
times, he was signed to race for former

F1 driver, Adrián Campos. He drove in the Spanish Euro Open MoviStar in 1999 and claimed victory in his second race for the team. In the following season, he was promoted to Formula 3000, where he joined Team Astromega as the youngest driver in the series. His F1 debut came at the Australian Grand Prix with Minardi in 2001.

After his historic victory in 2005, the following year saw Alonso on a definitive winning streak. He claimed the top prize in Bahrain and followed it up with wins in Australia, Monaco, Britain and Canada with Renault. He moved to McLaren in 2007, but signed once again with Renault at the end of the year, for a reputed £25 million.

THE A TO Z OF GRAND PRIX

Andretti

Active on the racing circuit between 1968 and 1972 and then in 1974 up to 1982, Mario Gabriele Andretti enjoyed a long and established career with Formula One. Born in Montona d'Istria in Italy on 28 February 1940, he was naturalised in the US in 1964 and became synonymous with speed in his adopted country. He is the only driver to be named United States Driver of the Year in three decades (1967, 1978 and 1984) and the only driver to win four times on road courses, paved ovals and dirt tracks in one season.

At a young age, Andretti and his twin brother Aldo were hired to park cars at a garage. It was here that Andretti became hooked on motors and he joined the Italian youth racing league at the age of 13. His debut in open wheel racing came in 1968 at the US Grand Prix at Watkins Glen. He was racing for Lotus under Colin Chapman.

Andretti was voted Driver of the Century in 2000 by Associated Press and *RACER* magazine as well as winning many other major awards. Today he still takes an active interest in racing from his home in Nazareth, Pennsylvania and is a popular speaker.

▲ Mario Andretti drives a John Player Special MK4 during the 1978 British Grand Prix.

◀ Mario Andretti at Brands Hatch for the 1970 British Grand Prix.

Ascari

The Italian racing driver Alberto
Ascari won the Formula One world
championship twice and is one of only
two Italians to do so throughout the
sport's history so far. Antonio Ascari, his
father, was himself a talented star on the
racetrack during the early 1920s. Ascari
senior was leading the French Grand
Prix in 1925 when he was killed, but

won nine Grands Prix in succession, but sadly his career was to be cut short in 1955 when he crashed a Ferrari at Monza. Out on the circuit in just shirt sleeves and a borrowed helmet he set out on 26 May to try a few test laps. Coming out of a fast curve on the third lap the car skidded and somersaulted twice throwing Ascari onto the track. He suffered multiple injuries and died where he fell. He was just 36 years old.

◀ Alberto Ascari toasts his victory in the 1952 British Grand Prix.

◀◀ Alberto Ascari in a Ferrari on his way to winning the Dutch Grand Prix in 1953.

▼ Alberto Ascari in the pits at Silverstone, 1950.

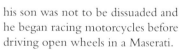

his son was not to be dissuaded and he began racing motorcycles before driving open wheels in a Maserati.

Born on 13 July 1918, his first Grand Prix win came in 1948 at Sanremo in Italy. His career went from strength to strength and he set the undefeated world record for the six fastest laps in succession during the 1952 world championship season. During that season and the next he

Australia

With 58 challenging laps and a total distance of 307.574 kilometres, the Melbourne Circuit in eastern Australia is a tough race for any driver. The Grand Prix has been a part of life in this sprawling country since 1928, but moved to the grand metropolis of Melbourne and its home in Albert Park in 1996. Since that time (apart from 2006) the city has hosted the first Grand Prix of the season each year.

Australia's racing history, like much of its culture, is fairly young in historic terms, however, for many years a road race around Albert Park did feature F1-style open wheel vehicles, which despite its lack of Grand Prix involvement, did attract top class drivers across the globe who eagerly competed with enthusiastic locals. Australia became part of the F1 world championship in 1985 and the first Grand Prix took place at the Adelaide Street Circuit in what would become traditionally (until the move to Melbourne) the last race of the season. Renowned for its party atmosphere, the Grand Prix in Adelaide was a favourite with drivers and spectators alike and was highly acclaimed as a road circuit.

Bahrain

In 2004, Michael Schumacher set the fastest lap time at 1:30.252 on a circuit length of 5.412 kilometres in Bahrain. Renowned for being one of the safest tracks in the world – thanks to its giant run-off areas – the Bahrain Grand Prix was sponsored by Gulf Air from its inaugural race in 2004 up until the end of the 2007 season.

Schumacher may have won the first Bahrain Grand Prix but Fernando Alonso won in 2005 and 2006.

Brazilian Felipe Massa won the 2007 Grand Prix on the circuit heavily criticised for its "safe" run-off areas where drivers are not penalised for straying from the track.

Traditionally, Bahrain hosts the third race of the season, in April (although it did host the season's first event in 2006). Work on the current circuit – the Sakhir track – began in 2002 and today

▲ Michael Schumacher crosses the line to win the Bahrain Grand Prix in 2004.

◄ Car racing round the Albert Park Circuit.

▼ The Bahrain Circuit showing the large run off areas.

it is also popular for its drag racing, F3, GT races and the Australian V8 Supercar series. However, in 2009, the Yas Island Circuit in Abu Dhabi is expected to take on the responsibility of hosting the Middle East Grand Prix.

▲ The start-finish straight at Francorchamps.

Belgium

Constructors Ferrari have enjoyed most wins in Belgium. The fastest lap was set in 2004 by Kimi Raikkonen when he completed the 7.004 kilometre circuit known as Circuit de Spa-Francorchamps in 1:45.108. Belgium's first national race took place in 1925 and the current track was built in 1929 to specifically accommodate the Grand Prix.

With unpredictable weather conditions, the circuit is a firm favourite on the racing calendar. Drivers often face clear conditions in one stretch of the track followed by rain and slippery surfaces in another. In fact, the circuit has suffered rain for 20 years in a row during its long established history and, as a result, is known as one of the most challenging courses of the season.

The inaugural race was won by the legendary Antonio Ascari in 1925 and this race has known its fair share of tragedies. In 1939, Richard "Dick" Seaman from Britain lost his life while in the lead and 21 years later, two drivers – Chris Bristow and Alan Stacey – died in separate accidents while competing in the Belgian Grand Prix.

Twelve years later, in 1972, the circuit was considered too dangerous for F1 racing and an alternative track at Nivelles was used. However, there was no challenge and little excitement and the race returned permanently to Spa in 1975.

Benetton

▼ Benetton
driver Michael
Schumacher
celebrates on
the podium
after winning the
Japanese Grand
Prix, 1995.

The company was founded in northern
Italy by Luciano Benetton, who chose
F1 as the vehicle to further promote
his fashion chain in 1986. Previously,
Benetton had sponsored the likes of
Tyrrell, Alfa Romeo and Toleman,

but gained so much satisfaction from
his involvement in the sport that he
bought the Toleman team and Benetton
Formula Ltd was born.

When Flavio Briatore was appointed
team boss in 1989 results were swift and
successful which was perhaps surprising
for a man who had no F1 experience.
However, his decision to involve TWR
brought major structural changes to the

◄ Alessandro Nannini in his Benetton Cosworth during the 1989 Brazilian Grand Prix.

team, and the arrival of a young Michael Schumacher was just the winning ingredient that Benetton required. Benetton quickly realised that they had a potential champion on their hands and were instrumental in shaping the young German's historical career.

In 1998, there were major changes for the team and Wurz and Fisichella were taken on as drivers. Both were lucky that season as Wurz suffered a nasty crash during the Canadian Grand Prix and Fisichella managed to escape his burning car in Belgium. Up until 2001, Benetton Formula Ltd was based in Chipping Norton and overseen by managing director Rocco Benetton. The team was bought by Renault in 2000 and at the start of the 2002 season changed their name to Renault F1.

BMW Sauber

In 2005, car manufacturer BMW made a successful takeover bid for the existing Sauber Formula One team and BMW Sauber made an impressive start to their championship campaign in 2006 when they finished in fifth place at the end of their first season. With bases in Switzerland and Germany, the team moved into second place at the end of the 2007 season and looked in a good position to equal that form the following year.

During the 1970s and 1980s, Peter Sauber competed in racing having built his first car in 1970. Becoming linked with Mercedes-Benz at the end of the 1980s, by 1993, the Swiss team were ready to face the trials and tribulations of F1 and the partnership with Mercedes supported them to the end of the following season. But, things were not happening on a major level for the team and their most successful campaign came in 2001 when they finished fourth in the constructors' championship.

Meanwhile, BMW were supplying engines between 1982-1987 and 2000-2005. In 2005, BMW ended its agreement with Williams to supply engines and bought Sauber. Nick Heidfeld and Robert Kubica were announced as team drivers in 2007. The team remained for 2008 and the F1.08 was launched in January that same year.

Brabham

Renowned racing driver Jack Brabham founded Motor Racing Developments in 1960 with fellow Australian Ron Tauranac. Generally known as Brabham, the company was the world's largest manufacturer of open wheel racing cars throughout the 1960s and built more than 500 cars in one decade.

The 1970s and 1980s brought unprecedented success with wins in Formula Two and Formula Three and two F1 drivers' championships in the 1980s with Nelson Piquet behind the wheel. They were also the first to win the world championship with a turbo-charged car. Brabham eventually won four drivers' championships and two constructors' world championships in its 30 years history, and Jack Brabham is still the only driver to win a championship in a car of which he was also the constructor, thanks to his 1966 victory.

The two founding members of Motor Racing

Developments Ltd did much to enhance the development of F1 and racing cars with their innovations such as the highly successful "fan-car" (although this was at first controversial) and in-race refuelling. They were also responsible for initiating the introduction of carbon brakes and the hydro-pneumatic suspension. Bernie Ecclestone owned the company throughout much of the 1970s and 1980s and began looking strategically at the commercial aspects of F1.

▼ Nelson Piquet in his Brabham BMW at Brands Hatch, 1983.

Brazil

▲ Giancarlo
Fisichella on a rain
soaked track at
Interlagos.
▶ The cars
negotiate a bend
at the start of the
2006 Brazilian
Grand Prix.

Pronounced in Portuguese as Grande
Prêmio do Brasil, the Brazilian Grand
Prix is held at the Autódromo José
Carlos Pace in Interlagos. The first
race took place here in 1972 although
was not included in the F1 world
championship calendar until a year later.
At 4.309 kilometres per lap, the circuit
is cited as one of the most exciting
and challenging courses of the season.
The 2003 Grand Prix was particularly
memorable for being Fisichella's first

major victory – a result which was
highly unexpected at the time due to
unforeseen circumstances caused by
heavy rain.

Another notable Brazilian Grand
Prix came two years later when, after

finishing in third place, Fernando Alonso gained enough points to become the youngest ever Formula One world champion, despite having two races still to go. In 2006, Brazil hosted the final race of the season when Michael Schumacher said goodbye to F1. The most wins at the circuit were gained by Alain Prost while the fastest lap was recorded by Juan Pablo Montoya at 1:11.473 when he won the 305.909 kilometre (71 lap) race in 2004.

Britain

The annual British Grand Prix was held on 6 July 2008 at the legendary Silverstone Circuit in Northamptonshire. As one of the oldest Grands Prix on the calendar, along with Italy, the race in the UK was first established by Henry Segrave in 1926 at Brooklands following his victory at the French Grand Prix three years earlier. In 1950, Silverstone hosted the first ever F1 world championship race and then went on to become the stalwart venue (the race alternated between Silverstone, Brands Hatch, and Aintree between 1964 and 1986). However, it has been the sole host of the event since 1987. The circuit was known as one of the fastest on the racing calendar until 1991 when the track was modified.

Despite some exciting wins at Silverstone for drivers including Mansell, Hill and Coulthard, the circuit's future was called into question in 2004 when it was left off the calendar due to an ongoing dispute over racing fees. The issue was finally resolved and the Grand

Prix will continue at Silverstone until
the end of the 2009 season before
moving to Donington Park. With a
race length of 308.46 kilometres, Jim
Clark and Alain Prost have clocked
up most wins at the circuit.

BRM

► A Marlboro BRM with Niki Lauda at the wheel.

▼ Jackie Stewart in his BRM in 1967.

The BRM team was a dominant force in racing between 1950 and 1977. Founded in 1945 by Raymond Mays and Peter Berthon, the company competed in 197 Grands Prix and recorded 17 wins,

a drivers' world championship with Graham Hill and was runner up in the constructors' championship on no less than four occasions. BRM can boast many famous drivers alongside Hill including the renowned Mike Hawthorn, Jackie Stewart, John Surtees, Niki Lauda, Reg Parnell and Dan Gurney to name but a few.

The founders, together with the highly regarded Sir Alfred Owen, entered BRM cars in F1 under the official name of the Owen Racing Organisation. Based in the small Lincolnshire village of Bourne, the company set up a factory on Spalding Road to build the extremely ambitious V16. Design problems were varied and eventually the vehicle was deemed unreliable (despite limited success) and they devised the Type 25. The company's turnaround came with chief engineer Tony Rudd, whose expertise and technical skills helped to lift the team's flagging status. However, Ferrari and other teams outshone BRM who faded from the limelight.

▼ Jenson Button in his 2008 Honda.

Button

Born in Frome, Somerset, on 19 January 1980, Jenson Alexander Lyons Button came to prominence on the F1 circuit in 2000. His racing career began in karting when he was just eight years old and at the age of 11 he won all 34 races of the British Cadet Kart Championship (including overall victory) in 1991. He followed up his success with three wins in the British Open Kart Championship and in 1997 became the youngest driver to win the European Super A Championship. He also won the Ayrton Senna Memorial Cup and his career in F1 seemed assured.

Supported by his father John Button, a renowned Rallycross driver, Button won nine races and the title in the British Formula Ford Championship at the tender age of 18. His first season in F1 saw him finish eighth overall and his potential was plain for all to see. Under contract with Williams, Button drove for Benetton (in their first year with Renault) but failed to find his winning form. At the start of the 2006 season Button was driving for the newly formed Honda Racing F1 where he

claimed his first Grand Prix victory in Hungary. Partnering Barrichello for Honda in 2007, Button was – despite a miserable season – to remain an integral part of the team for 2008.

▲ Jenson Button on the podium after winning the 2006 Hungarian Grand Prix.

Canada

Known in French as the Grand Prix du Canada, the Canadian Grand Prix has been held in the country since the early 1960s. It officially joined the world championships in 1967 where it hosted the first F1 race at Mosport Park in Bowmanville, Ontario. The event was then alternated between Mosport

Park and Circuit Mont-Tremblant in Quebec before safety concerns moved the race permanently to Mosport.

The first F1 Grand Prix was won by Canadian Gilles Villeneuve – father of Jacques – who was sadly killed in qualifying for the Belgian Grand Prix. The Montreal Circuit was then named in his honour following his death in

◀ Crowds watch a practice session at the Canadian Circuit.

◀◀ Lewis Hamilton on his way to his first Grand Prix victory in Canada, 2007.

1982, however, another serious accident on the track occurred a month later when his team-mate Didier Pironi stalled on the grid. Clipped by the car behind and shunted into the car in front, Pironi was flown to hospital but later died from his injuries.

The circuit would also witness happier times and Jean Alesi had an emotional win at Mosport in 1995; it would be the only win of a long established career. Having endured a rough season the year before, Alesi was a firm favourite with the crowd and his victory was voted the most popular of the season. Lewis Hamilton secured his first Grand Prix victory in Montreal in 2007.

China

The Shanghai International Circuit is the setting for the Chinese Grand Prix with its 56 laps of 5.451 kilometres. In 2004, Michael Schumacher set the fastest lap here at 1:32.238. Traditionally, the Chinese Grand Prix is set towards the end of the season in October.

The idea for a Grand Prix in China has its roots in the early 1990s when the Chinese government were looking to build a circuit in Zhuhai in the Guangdong Province of southern China. However, the purpose-built track failed to meet FIA standards and hopes to enter the 1999 world championships were abandoned. Hope within the government didn't wane and with help from the Macau Grand Prix's organisers the first Chinese F1 race took place in 2004 following an agreement between the Shanghai International Circuit and the FIA.

Barrichello was the first Grand Prix winner that year followed by new world champion Fernando Alonso in 2005. The 2006 title went to Michael Schumacher; it would be his last victory before his retirement from Formula One. Kimi Raikkonen won the 2007 Chinese Grand Prix and Ferrari can claim three constructors' wins at the circuit.

Clark

James "Jim" Clark Junior, was born on 4 March 1936 in Fife, Scotland, the youngest of five children. Active in F1 between 1960 and 1968, he was the dominant driver of his time having won more Grand Prix races than any other. He claimed a total of 25 victories and two world championship titles.

His career began in rallying and hill climbs where he drove his own car – a Talbot Sunbeam. His winning results and a meeting with Colin Chapman set Clark on the road to glory but his

career wasn't without its problems. During one of his first Grand Prix races in Italy in 1961, Clark was hit in his Lotus by von Trips in a Ferrari. The Ferrari became airborne and von Trips was flung from the car. He and 15 spectators were sadly killed.

Clark continued to achieve success and in 1963 he won seven of the 10 F1 races and took his first drivers' world championship while Lotus won its first constructors' title. On 7 April 1968, Jim Clark was killed instantly when his Lotus veered off the track at Hockenheimring in Germany and crashed into nearby trees.

◀ Jim Clark talking to Lotus mechanics before a race.

▼ Jim Clark taking the chequered flag at the 1963 British Grand Prix at Silverstone.

Coulthard

▶ On the podium after winning in Portugal, 1995.

▼ David Coulthard's Red Bull car for the 2008 season.

It all began, like many others, in karting for David Marshall Coulthard who moved into Formula Ford in 1989. The young Scot, born on 27 March 1971, was extremely impressive and went on to win the McLaren/Autosport Young Driver of the Year award. He was employed as a test driver for Williams–Renault in 1993 and was instrumental in developing the car's technology. He stayed in the job for a further year but, following the tragic death of Ayrton Senna, was promoted to team driver alongside Damon Hill for the Spanish

Grand Prix. He stepped aside for Nigel Mansell on four occasions but became a full-time driver for Williams in 1995.

Coulthard's first Grand Prix win came that same year in Portugal but otherwise he had a fairly uneventful first full season. In 1996 he moved to McLaren where his season lacked magic and for the next few years it seemed that he was stuck in a supporting role. His career was granted no favours when the FIA introduced the single-lap qualifying format. Coulthard found it hard to work to this format. He moved to Red Bull Racing in 2005 where he stayed for 2006 and 2007. He was contracted to stay with Red Bull until the end of 2008 because of his experience.

De Cesaris

Multiple karting champion Andrea de Cesaris graduated to Formula Three in the UK where he proved his potential by winning numerous races. Born in Rome on 31 May 1959, the talented Italian was renowned for his wild reputation and reckless approach to racing. Despite this he was promoted to Formula Two and was chosen by Alfa Romeo in 1980 to become a team driver for the world championship in place of Vittorio Brambilla.

His F1 debut came in Canada at the age of 21, however, his first Grand Prix was short lived. Engine failure saw the young de Cesaris out of the race after just eight laps. His second Grand Prix in the US was equally disappointing when he crashed on lap two. The Italian went on, however, to have a 14-year F1 career and the change in fortune came about with an initial move to McLaren in 1981. A year later he was back with Alfa Romeo having earned himself the nickname of "Andrea de Crasheris"; he had spun off the track and crashed on six occasions in just 14 races. Despite a long career, de Cesaris never really took off in F1, although he did record some decent results.

▲ Another disappointment for Andrea de Cesaris as his Brabham BMW catches fire.

▼ Andrea de Cesaris in action in his Ligier Renault, 1984.

Ecclestone

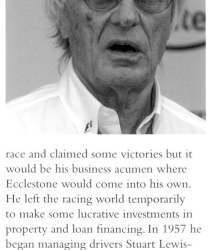

▶ Formula One
supremo Bernie
Ecclestone.

▼ Bernie
Ecclestone
larking around
with Michael
Schumacher.

Considered the primary authority in Formula One racing, Bernard "Bernie" Charles Ecclestone was born in Suffolk on 28 October 1930. He is president and CEO of Formula One Management and Formula One Administration and also owns a stake in Alpha Prema, the parent company of the Formula One Group of companies.

Often referred to as the "F1 Supremo" by journalists, Ecclestone's early career was as a competitor and began in 1949. After a collision with a fellow competitor at Brands Hatch he continued to race and claimed some victories but it would be his business acumen where Ecclestone would come into his own. He left the racing world temporarily to make some lucrative investments in property and loan financing. In 1957 he began managing drivers Stuart Lewis-Evans and Jochen Rindt before buying Brabham in 1972. He remained with the company for almost 20 years.

Ecclestone is renowned for his business insight and negotiating skills. He was ranked the third richest person in the UK in 2003 in the *Sunday Times Rich List* and sold one of his London residences for £57.1 million to a steel magnate. This made the house the most expensive ever sold.

Europe

Re-introduced during the mid-1980s, the European Grand Prix is a separate event in the Formula One calendar which has been held regularly since 1999. With 56 laps and a total race length of 306.488 kilometres, the 2007 race was won by Fernando Alonso in a McLaren-Mercedes in just over two hours and six minutes. It was announced in 2007 that, from the following year, the European Grand Prix would take place for at least a further seven years.

The race was created as an honorary title by the FIA's predecessor, the AIACR, and the first to receive the title was the Italian Grand Prix back in 1923. It was then given to the French Grand Prix, followed by the Belgian Grand Prix but the final title of the era was given to Spa in 1930 before the onset of the Second World War.

The European Grand Prix was resurrected in 1947 and remained an important part of the racing calendar until 1977 (where the last country to receive the title was Britain). There were no further plans for the event until 1983 when the New York Grand Prix was cancelled and Brands Hatch quickly took its place. It was replaced in 1986 by the Hungarian Grand Prix, but Bernie Ecclestone brought the event back to the UK in 1992 with a planned event at Donington. In 2008, the European Grand Prix took place in Valencia, Spain.

▼ Mark Webber driving through the street circuit of Valencia in 2008.

▼ Alain Prost
takes the lead
in the 1993
European Grand
Prix at Donington.

Fangio

A ctive in Formula One between 1950–1951 and 1953–1958, Juan Manuel Fangio was born in Argentina on 24 June 1911. Nicknamed "The Master", Fangio would dominate the first 10 years of Formula One racing, winning five drivers' championships which stood as a record for 46 years. His incredible talent on the circuit has seen Fangio cited as perhaps "the greatest driver of all time". He was Argentine National Champion in 1940 and 1941 and began his racing career in Europe seven years later. But, interestingly, he came to racing relatively later in life and was often the oldest competitor on the track.

Racing against the likes of Alberto Ascari and Stirling Moss amongst others, Fangio was racing at a time when protective clothing and equipment were still in their infancy and F1 was

▲ Juan Manuel Fangio at Silverstone .

a particularly dangerous sport. His F1 debut came in 1948 at the French Grand Prix. It was the only race in F1 for the Argentinian that season but in 1949 he entered six F1 races and won four. Having retired from racing, Fangio was kidnapped by Cuban rebels in 1958. He was later released and in a surprise move became firm friends with his captors. He died at the age of 84 in Buenos Aires in 1995.

F

FARINA

▶ Farina with his
pit crew.

▼ Giuseppe
Farina taking the
chequered flag
at the Argentine
Grand Prix in 1953.

Farina

Emilio Giuseppe "Nino" Farina was born in Turin, Italy, on 30 October 1906 and made his mark on Formula One when he became the first ever drivers' world champion in 1950. Known as Nino, Farina was renowned for his "straight–arm" style of driving and began his career in hill climbs. He graduated to circuit racing driving a Maserati and things really took off for the young Italian when he moved to Alfa Romeo partnering the legendary Tazio Nuvolari. He came into his own during the late 1930s with notable wins in minor races and he was the Italian Drivers' Champion in 1937, 1938 and 1939.

The Second World War temporarily brought his career to an end for eight years, however, in 1948 he won the Monaco Grand Prix and two years later reached the pinnacle of his career with his championship title. Three years later he won his final race at the 1953 German Grand Prix. And, in 1955, he raced in his last Grand Prix in Italy having taken painkillers to get him through following a

starting line crash the previous year which left the Italian badly burnt when his car caught fire. He retired after the Indianapolis 500 in 1956.

Ferrari

▲ Kimi Raikkonen in his 2008 Scuderia Ferrari.

▶ Michael Schumacher on the starting grid with his team members.

Scuderia Ferrari is the part of the Ferrari automobile company concerned with racing. Based in Maranello, Italy, Ferrari is headed by team principal Stefano Domenicali with team drivers Kimi Raikkonen and Felipe Massa. The company was founded in 1929 and raced for Alfa Romeo up to 1939. The team first competed in Formula One in 1948, during the sport's revival

following the Second World War and, today, Ferrari is possibly the oldest and one of the most successful competitors in the championship. The team won both the drivers' (Raikkonen) and constructors' titles in 2007.

The first race at Albert Park was a success for Ferrari, however, they had a disappointing time in Malaysia before faring better in Bahrain. At the Chinese Grand Prix, Ferrari achieved its 200th Formula One victory and its 599th

THE A TO Z OF GRAND PRIX

and 600th podium finishes. The team, overall, has had unparalleled success in Formula One and has won the most constructors' and driver championships as well as recording the most wins of all time. Ferrari also have the honour of having the most wins in one season and the most podium appearances as well as most pole positions and most points of all time in the history of F1.

F

Fisichella

Born in Rome on 14 January 1973,
Giancarlo Fisichella – known as
"Fisi" – is the renowned Italian driver
for Force India. He began his career
in karting before being promoted to
the Italian Formula Three series. He
finished the season as runner up for
the RC Motorsport team in 1993 and
went on to win the championship
the following year. He left the sport
for a brief time in 1995 when he
joined the International Touring Car

Championship for Alfa Romeo, but
made his debut in Formula One in
1996 for Minardi. The team required
a driver with funding and Fisichella
found himself replaced by Giovanni
Lavaggi before the end of the season.

Undeterred, he signed for Jordan
in 1997 where he partnered Ralf
Schumacher and stood on the F1
podium for the first time at the
Canadian Grand Prix. His capabilities
brought him to the attention of the
Benetton team who signed him for
the 1998 season. He remained with
the team until 2001 but found life
tough in the changing
environment and
Benetton's traditionally
poor second half of the
season. He made the
move back to Jordan in
2002 before signing with
Sauber in 2004. He spent
his subsequent seasons
with Renault partnering
Alonso. He became lead
driver following his
team-mate's departure in
2007 and moved to Force
India in 2008 to partner
Adrian Sutil.

Fittipaldi

The highly talented Brazilian, Emerson Fittipaldi, made his Formula One debut in the 1970 season having been "discovered" by Colin Chapman. Born on 12 December 1946, he was active in the sport for 10 years and won the drivers' world championship twice, in 1972 and 1974. He began racing motorcycles at the age of 14 and, after his brother survived a crash on a hydrofoil, decided to try his hand at kart racing. Fittipaldi and his brother Wilson raced Formula Vees and together

▲ Emerson Fittipaldi (centre) in discussion with Colin Chapman (left), designer and owner of Lotus Cars.

◀ Emerson Fittipaldi rounding a bend at Brands Hatch on his way to winning in 1972.

with their parents built up a company. Fittipaldi went on to win the Brazilian Formula Vee title aged 21 and moved to Europe in 1969 confident that he would find a team to take him on. He had a winning formula that Chapman found encouraging and he was signed for Lotus partnering Jochen Rindt.

When Rindt was killed at Monza, Fittipaldi found himself as first team driver and he finished sixth in the drivers' championship in 1971.

His career went from strength to strength and he left Lotus to join the up and coming McLaren team in 1974. He shocked the racing fraternity when he left McLaren to join his brother's team, Fittipaldi Automotive, where he remained for an unexciting five seasons. He retired from F1 in 1980 at the age of 33. He was inducted into the Motorsports Hall of Fame of America in 2001.

THE A TO Z OF GRAND PRIX

Force India

Founded in October 2007, Force India is based at Silverstone in Northamptonshire. Under the guidance of team principal Colin Kolles, the race drivers comprise Adrian Sutil and Giancarlo Fisichella supported by test drivers Vitantonio Liuzzi, Roldan Rodriguez and Giedo van der Garde. The team made their Formula One debut in the 2008 season which, with Delhi set to host the first ever Indian Grand Prix in 2010, increased the country's participation in the F1 calendar.

Originally called Spyker, a consortium led by Vijay Mallya and Michiel Mol bought the team for 88 million euros in 2007 and the FIA agreed the name change to Force India on 24 October. Michiel Mol remained director of F1 racing with chief technology officer Mike Gascoyne. The team use an updated version of the Spyker car with a VJM01 chassis and a Ferrari engine (Force India's deal will run until 2010). The Indian flag

▲ Force India team drivers at their launch in 2008.

appears in the team logo and Force India construct their own cars as Spyker did before them. The team is sponsored by Kingfisher, ICICI Bank, Medion, Samsung and others and has partnership arrangements with Airbus and EADS who provide technical support.

France

With 70 laps and a race distance of 308.586 kilometres, the Circuit de Nevers Magny-Cours plays host to the French Grand Prix. It was in France that the first Grand Prix took place and the country is proud of its long and established history of motor racing.

Several tracks have been used for the Grand Prix including the Autodrome de Montlhéry but, since 1991, the permanent home for this prestigious event has been Magny-Cours.

The move to the current circuit had a lot to do with the local economy; it was hoped to improve the area, however, it is fairly remote and many of those involved in F1 often complain of the circuit's isolation. The troubles don't end there. In 2004 and 2005 there was some doubt about whether the French Grand Prix would take place due to financial issues and new and up and coming additions to the F1 calendar.

Although the races did take place as planned, the circuit's future remained in the balance and in March 2007 it was announced that the French F1 event would be suspended due to ongoing financial implications. But, in a surprise move, the 2008 French Grand Prix was indeed hosted at Magny-Cours although the 2009 race was cancelled in October 2008.

◀ Felipe Massa wins at Magny-Cours, 2008.

▼ A section of the pits at Magny-Cours.

Germany

In 1907, the Taunus Circuit played host to the first of Germany's *Kaiserpreis* races, the inaugural race being won by the Italian Felice Nazzaro. Today, the German Grand Prix is held at Hockenheimring and consists of 67 laps with a total race distance of 306.46 kilometres.

Germany's history in the sport has been somewhat controversial due to the Second World War and, for a time, the country was banned from international events. However, in 1951, Germany was allowed to join the Formula One calendar and the annual Grand Prix was held at the Solitude Circuit in Stuttgart. In 1970, drivers demanded some safety improvements and modifications at the circuit. The request came too late and, as a result, the Grand Prix was moved to Hockenheimring (its current venue) which had already been modified.

The German Grand Prix had also been held at the Nordschleife Circuit in Nurburgring, but Niki Lauda's crash on the track in the 1970s sealed the alternative venue's fate. Hockenheimring became the agreed permanent home of the F1 race in 1977. In 1995, the new track at Nurburgring, "Grand Prix Strecke", was introduced on the calendar and between 2007 and 2010 it will be used as an alternative venue.

▲ The Hockenheimring in 1990.

◀ The starting grid at Hockenheimring.

H

Hakkinen

▼ Mika Hakkinen takes the flag in his McLaren-Mercedes to win the Austrian Grand Prix, 1998.

B etween 1991 and 2001 the name Mika Hakkinen was synonymous with motor racing. Born in Finland on 28 September 1968, Hakkinen won 20 Grand Prix races throughout his career,

clocking up a total of 420 points with 51 podium appearances. It all started on the go-kart track for the young Finnish lad from Vantaa where he won five karting championships by 1986. Other championship wins followed including the British Formula Three and F1 Lotus sat up and took notice. He was signed to Lotus in 1991 and made his debut in Phoenix in the US.

Hakkinen was partnered by Johnny Herbert from 1992 and his form continued to shine. He finished the drivers' championship in a respectable eighth place. He joined McLaren as test driver in 1993 and was promoted to team driver. When Ayrton Senna left McLaren for Williams in 1994,

Hakkinen found himself as lead driver alongside Martin Brundle.

By 1998, with his first win under his belt, Hakkinen looked set for stardom by winning the world championship. He followed it up with a second title in 1999 despite tough competition from Eddie Irvine. By 2001, Hakkinen's McLaren wasn't as competitive but despite this his form remained strong although it proved to be his last season in F1.

◄ Mika Hakkinen stands on his car in the pit lane after winning the 1999 Canadian Grand Prix.

▼ Mika Hakkinen leads the pack at the start of the British Grand Prix, 1998.

which gave the option of a future F1 seat. Hamilton took the challenge enthusiastically and it was announced in November 2006 that he would represent the team alongside Alonso.

He finished third in Australia and became the 14th driver to make the podium on a debut. He continued in style and ended the races in Bahrain and Spain in second place. This gave him the lead in the championship and made him the youngest driver to do so. He again finished second in Monaco (behind team-mate Alonso)

Hamilton

▲ Lewis Hamilton making his podium debut at the Australian Grand Prix, 2007.

▶ Lewis Hamilton during a pit stop on his way to winning the Canadian Grand Prix in 2007

Hailing from Stevenage in Hertfordshire, Lewis Carl Davidson Hamilton was born on 7 January 1985. His explosive career has catapulted the young Brit into the limelight from the start and, since making his debut in the Australian Grand Prix in 2007, he has set numerous rookie records. Having enjoyed unprecedented success in karting he was signed to the McLaren driver development programme

but claimed his first victory in Canada. He repeated his win at the US Grand Prix, and together with Jacques Villeneuve is the second rookie to win more than one race in a first season. He went on to win the Hungarian Grand Prix and the race in Japan before eventually losing out by one point on the championship to Kimi Raikkonen (as did Alonso) at the end of the 2007 season. The 2008 campaign, however, saw Hamilton emerge victorious and eclipse Alonso's achievement as the youngest ever F1 champion.

▼ Lewis Hamilton leads the pack at the start of the Belgian Grand Prix, September 2008.

Hawthorn

In 1958, John Michael "Mike" Hawthorn claimed his first and only championship victory. Born on 10 April 1929, Hawthorn's debut came at the Belgian Grand Prix in 1952. The Yorkshireman finished in an extremely respectable fourth place which was the best Grand Prix debut by any British world champion before the arrival of Lewis Hamilton. He eventually raced to his first win eight races later at the 1953 French Grand Prix at Reims. He started 45 races throughout his career (having qualified for 47) and won a total of three Grands Prix. He claimed 18 podium finishes and found himself in pole position on four occasions.

Sadly, for Hawthorn, his win at the 1955 24 hours Le Mans race was overshadowed by a horrific crash which killed 82 spectators. Despite winning only one Grand Prix in 1958, his points were enough to secure the drivers' championship, although he then announced his retirement from Formula One. His last race came at the 1958 Moroccan Grand Prix. His retirement was short-lived.

On 22 January 1959, Hawthorn was involved in an accident on the A3 in Surrey. He died as a result of his injuries. Since 1959 the Hawthorn Memorial Trophy has been awarded to the most successful British or Commonwealth Formula One driver each year.

THE A TO Z OF GRAND PRIX

Hill

Born on 17 September 1960 in London, Damon Hill followed in his father's footsteps when he made his debut in Formula One in 1992. He had signed for Williams as a test driver in 1991 and a year later joined the ailing Brabham team at the age of 32. It was considered a fairly late age to begin a high-profile career in motor sport but Hill proved himself more than worthy of the challenge.

Initially he partnered Alain Prost at Williams (from 1993) and after a disappointing first half of the season went on to secure victories in Hungary, Belgium and Italy. His third consecutive win for Williams clinched the team the constructors' title that year (while Prost took the drivers' championship). The following year saw the legendary Ayrton Senna joining Hill at Williams where he

◀ Success for Damon Hill at Monza in 1993.

▼ Jordan driver Damon Hill celebrates his racing career after announcing his retirement in 1999.

▲ Damon Hill drives through a chicane to win at Catalunya in 1994.

retained his "0" number on his car for the second season running; he was only the second driver in Formula One to be given the number.

When Senna died at Imola, Hill found himself in the top driving seat with only one season's experience behind him. David Coulthard was brought in to partner Hill who went on to take an emotional victory in Spain just two races later. In 1996 he won the championship. He enjoyed many on-track battles with Michael Schumacher but retired from racing in 1999.

Hill

Twice drivers' world champion, Graham Hill had a prolific career on the track between 1958 and 1975. His debut in Formula One came at the 1958 Monaco Grand Prix. Hill would go on to claim 14 victories, 36 podium finishes (from his 179 races) and would score a total of 270 points. Having come across an advert for racing at Brands Hatch, Hill made his debut on a circuit in 1954 where he paid five shillings per lap. Driving a Cooper 500 Formula Three car he became hooked and was soon taken on by Lotus as a mechanic. He persuaded his new team to try him in the driving seat.

By 1960 he had joined BRM and rewarded his team with a championship victory two years later. Seven years followed and Hill once again joined Lotus. When Jim Clark and Mike Spence were killed, Hill became first choice driver and won his second title in 1968. His legs were broken in an accident in the US in 1969 but he was soon back in F1. Despite a comeback, Hill's career didn't prove as successful as it had been previously and his last

◀ Graham Hill in contemplative mood.

▼ Graham Hill in his BRM taking the chequered flag in Monte Carlo, 1965.

race came at the 1975 Grand Prix in Monaco. Hill was killed when piloting a plane which crashed in foggy conditions in north London in November 1975.

Hill

▲ Phil Hill at the wheel of his Ferrari, Monaco 1961.

▲▲ Crowds turn out to see Phil Hill celebrate his Monza win.

Philip Toll Hill Junior, born on 20 April 1927, was the only American-born driver to win the F1 championship which he achieved in 1961. His debut in Formula One came at the French Grand Prix in 1958 having moved to the UK as a trainee for Jaguar in 1949. He signed for Ferrari in 1956. The same year that he made his debut driving a

Maserati, he also won the Le Mans 24 hours race with Olivier Gendebien (a winning formula that would see the two team-mates win the race on two more occasions). His 1961 championship was secured by winning the Grand Prix at Monza in Italy – the same race in which team-mate von Trips was killed.

He switched to Team ATS in 1962, following the engineer walkout, and stayed in the sport for a further five years. His final race in F1 was the 1966 Italian Grand Prix after which he moved into sports car racing. Following his retirement from F1, Hill went on to restore classic cars and was a television commentator as well as building up a long and established relationship with *Road & Track* magazine.

Honda

Based in Brackley in the UK, Team Honda had their first season in Formula One in 1964. Currently working with drivers Button and Barrichello and test drivers Conway and Wurz, the team use a Honda RA808E engine with tyres provided by Bridgestone Potenza. Despite never having won a constructors' world championship, Honda have seen two pole positions and two fastest laps though the 2007 season presented its fair share of problems.

On Honda's debut in 1964, they entered F1 with a single car which raced in the German, US and Italian Grands Prix and in the following year the team moved from Tokyo to Europe. During the latter half of the 1965 season, Honda employed two vehicles and scored their

▲ John Surtees in a Honda RA301 at the British Grand Prix, July 1968.

▲ Jenson Button's Honda for the 2008 season.

▶ Denny Hulme.

first point at the French Grand Prix. The first win for the team came in Mexico that same year thanks to American driver Richie Ginther. By 1968 Honda's success was on the increase with podium appearances by John Surtees (also the same year that they scored their first pole position).

Following success as engine suppliers during the 1980s and 1990s, the team was reformed for the start of the 2006 season where they scored a victory in the Hungarian Grand Prix. The 2007 season was more disappointing when aerodynamic and reliability problems put paid to any championship ambitions. Ross Brawn was appointed team principal for the 2008 season.

Hulme

Racing first for Brabham and then McLaren, Denis Clive "Denny" Hulme made his F1 debut at the Monaco Grand Prix in 1965. Born on 18 June 1936 in New Zealand, Hulme worked in a garage and saved enough money to buy an MG TF which he entered in hill climb races. He was subsequently chosen for the driver to Europe programme and became a mechanic in Brabham's garage where he began planning a career in F1.

He raced for Tyrrell in 1961 and rejoined Brabham for his debut in the mid-1960s. But, his first full season in F1 came in 1966 where he was second driver to Jack Brabham. In 1967, Hulme went on to win the championship five points ahead of Brabham and 10 ahead of Jim Clark. After retiring from F1 in 1974, he joined the Grand Prix Drivers' Association before retiring to his native New Zealand. In 1992, while driving at the Bathurst 1000 in Australia, he suffered a massive heart attack behind the wheel and died on the track. He was the first former F1 champion to die of natural causes.

1986 when he organised the first
F1 race behind the Iron Curtain
which attracted more than 200,000
spectators. The major coup pulled off by
Ecclestone was to become an amazing
success story and the event didn't even
see any rain until the 2006 Grand Prix.

The track is narrow, twisting and
often dusty (due to its under utilisation
as its considered a "professional"
circuit only) and provides the drivers
with immense challenges from the
off. The total race length is 306.663
kilometres and consists of 70 laps of
4.381 kilometres. The fastest lap time
was achieved by Michael Schumacher in
2004 in 1:19.071.

Hungary

▲ Ayrton Senna
taking part in the
Hungarian Grand
Prix, 1986.

▶ The
Hungaroring
Circuit set in a
natural valley.

Traditionally held in August, the
Hungarian Grand Prix takes place at
the Hungaroring Circuit in Budapest.
The first Grand Prix in the country
was held in 1936 and was attended by
a huge crowd eager to see the likes
of Mercedes-Benz, Auto Union and
Ferrari competing for pole position.
Sadly, politics, the Second World War
and other events brought Grand Prix
racing in Hungary to an abrupt end for
an incredible 50 years.

Bernie Ecclestone was the
mastermind that changed all that in

Hunt

James Simon Wallis Hunt was born on 29 August 1947 in Sutton, Surrey, and went on to become world champion in 1976. Originally destined for the medical profession, Hunt changed his mind approaching his 18th birthday when he was taken to see a race and became instantly hooked on the sport. He built a racing Mini and graduated to Formula Ford and F3 but soon acquired the nickname "Hunt the Shunt" for his aggressive tail-gating style which often resulted in spectacular accidents.

He signed for Lord Hesketh's team which at the time were not taken particularly seriously by the racing fraternity, however, Hunt's undeniable talent saw the up and coming champion thrive. His first Grand Prix win came in the Netherlands in 1975 and he finished in fourth place overall in the championship. When Lord Hesketh ran out of funds and sponsorship failed to materialise for his maverick team, Hunt signed for McLaren for the start of the 1976 season. It would prove to be the driver's best year and he won the drivers' world championship by one point.

Also renowned for his behaviour off the track (as much as on it), Hunt would famously attend top events in a T-shirt and jeans and was often barefoot. Hunt died at his home in Wimbledon, London, of a heart attack at the age of 45 in 1993.

▲ James Hunt taking a breather.

▼ Hunt, car 11, avoids getting involved in this pile up.

Italy

The Monza track in its beautiful setting.

Rubens Barrichello at Monza in 2004 when he set the fastest lap record.

The Italian Grand Prix takes place at the Monza Circuit and has a total race distance of 306.720 kilometres. With 53 laps of 5.793 kilometres, the fastest lap time recorded (1:21.046) was by Rubens Barrichello in 2004. It is one of the oldest events on the F1 calendar as the first Grand Prix here took place in 1921 in Brescia. Autodromo Nazionale Monza was built in time for the second race in 1922 and has remained the dominant circuit for the event ever since.

The 1923 Grand Prix was the scene of a rare European appearance by Harry A Miller who brought his "American Miller 122" for the event with driver Count Louis Zborowski who competed in the single seater. The most constructors' wins at Monza have

been recorded by Ferrari, although the 2007 winner was Fernando Alonso driving a McLaren-Mercedes.

The track was one of the inaugural Formula One championship races in 1950. Most driver victories have been secured by Michael Schumacher (five wins) who announced his retirement from F1 at Monza in 2006. Nelson Piquet has enjoyed four wins at the track while numerous other F1 stars, including Stirling Moss and Alain Prost, have achieved no less than three victories in the Italian Grand Prix.

J

Jaguar

Jaguar Racing competed in the F1 championship between 2000 and 2004 and was formed when Ford bought Jackie Stewart's team in 1999. As part of global marketing, the team was renamed Jaguar in an attempt to

promote the Jaguar car company. The team took part in 85 races in total but failed to win any championships – either for constructors or drivers. The best result they achieved was seventh in the constructors' race for 2002-2004 while their best driver result came with Eddie Irvine in 2002 who finished ninth overall in the championship.

The team's debut came at the start of

◀ Christian Klien in his Jaguar in 2004.

◀◀ Eddie Irvine, the most successful Jaguar driver.

the 2000 season in the Australian Grand Prix in Melbourne. However, despite the best efforts of Irvine, team-mate Johnny Herbert and the expertise of Wolfgang Reitzle, Jaguar never achieved the success under Ford that Stewart's team had enjoyed in the 1999 season. Reitzle stepped down in favour of Bobby Rahal for the start of the 2001 season, but even the successful team owner and former American racing champion were unable to improve results. Niki Lauda also failed to bring about a change in form and 2002 was a further disappointment for the team. Funding was reduced and Lauda and 70 other staff were made redundant in 2003. The final race for team Jaguar was the 2004 Brazilian Grand Prix after which it was bought by Red Bull.

Japan

The Japanese Grand Prix takes place at the Fuji Speedway Circuit in October in the F1 racing calendar. Felipe Massa set the fastest lap record here in 2008 with a time of 1:18.426 on the 4.563 kilometre circuit. The total race distance is 305.416 kilometres over 67 laps at this highly-popular event. The Suzuka Circuit, which was traditionally home to the F1 race, is an exciting and challenging course and has witnessed its fair share of championship wins and losses.

In 1994 and 1995, the Japanese Grand Prix was one of only six countries to host more than one Grand Prix in the same year; the others include Britain, Spain, Germany, the US and Italy. For 2007 and 2008, it was decided to hold the race at the Fuji Speedway Circuit – the country's site chosen for their inaugural Grand Prix in 1976. The current track was redesigned and from 2009 onwards will alternate with the Suzuka Circuit. The driver to win most victories in Japan is Michael Schumacher with six. During the late 1960s and early 1970s, native Motoharu Kurosawa was celebrated for his two wins in the Japanese Grand Prix.

▲ Lewis Hamilton in treacherous conditions.

◀ A view of the track in the foothills of Mount Fuji.

attention of Frank Williams but failed to create the magic the team were looking for. However, he was solid and reliable and in 1979 was putting himself, and the Williams team, firmly on the map with four wins in just five races. He finished the season in third place overall and was looking forward to an exciting 1980 campaign. He didn't disappoint and took the championship with a clear 13 points over fellow competitor Nelson Piquet. He retired after the 1981 season to take up a career in the Australian Touring Car Championship.

Jones

▲ Williams Ford driver Alan Jones in action at the British Grand Prix in 1980.

▶ A garlanded Alan Jones after his win at Brands Hatch, 1980.

Former Australian driver Alan Jones was born on 2 November 1946 and was the first to win a Formula One world championship with the Williams team. Jones' start in racing was fairly methodical. He stayed in Formula Three for nearly six years before his then team owner bought a car from Lord Hesketh, giving Jones the opportunity to leapfrog into F1. Formula Atlantic decided not to stay in F1 after just four races and he joined Graham Hill's racing team. However, his first full-time role in F1 came with John Surtees' team in 1976.

By 1977 he had come to the

Katayama

Japanese driver Ukyo Katayama was born in Tokyo on 29 May 1963 and tried, like many others from his native country, to make it big in the world of F1. Despite his lack of expertise and failure to make a huge impact out on the circuit, Katayama was popular for other reasons, namely his self-depreciating sense of humour and his incredibly sunny disposition. He headed for Europe at the start of his career where he raced in France during 1986 before heading back to Japan where he went on to win the Japanese F3000 in 1991.

He first joined F1 with the Larrousse team and impressed the racing fraternity with fifth position in the Canadian Grand Prix in 1992, however his engine blew and two embarrassing collisions with team-mate Bertrand Gachot saw his season end on a low note. In 1993 he moved to Tyrrell and attracted attention more for his constant accidents than for his driving. In 1994, however, it was Katayama's year and he was impressive as he left team-mate Mark Blundell behind. After two more seasons with the team Katayama suddenly lost his earlier form. After retiring from F1 he announced that he was suffering from cancer and, although not life-threatening, it was completely debilitating. Today, the ever popular Katayama is a commentator on Fuji TV for Formula One in Japan.

▲ Ukyo Katayama posing for his Tyrrell Yamaha team photograph.

Lauda

Three times world champion Andreas Nikolaus "Niki" Lauda was born in Vienna, Austria, on 22 February 1949. He moved quickly into Formula Vee and soon bought his way into March as a Formula Two driver for the fledgling team. In 1972 he was promoted to F1 for the team who suffered a catastrophic season that year. He again, took out a bank loan, and bought his way into the BRM team the following year but was then headhunted by Ferrari on the recommendation of former team-mate Clay Ragazzoni. The signing for Ferrari cleared Lauda's bank loans and he found the team had tremendous faith in his abilities despite his disappointing start to the season.

He won the 1975 world championship and looked set to win

a second in 1976 but disaster struck and Lauda was badly injured in Germany. He lapsed into a coma and was even read his last rites, however, Lauda – despite his horrific injuries and badly burned body – returned to take the championship title in 1977 and 1984. Today Lauda commentates on F1 for Austria and Germany on television and is heavily quoted in the international media. He was inducted into the International Motorsports Hall of Fame in 1993.

Lotus

▲ Stirling Moss in a Lotus 18, with the side panels taken out, on his way to winning the Monaco Grand Prix in 1961.

Renowned for encouraging its customers to race its cars, Lotus joined F1 with its own team in 1958. Just two years later, with Stirling Moss behind the wheel, the team won its first Grand Prix in Monaco in a Lotus 18. The Lotus 25 proved invaluable in 1962 and the following year – this time with Jim Clark – the team went on to win its first constructors' title. When Jim Clark crashed an F2 Lotus 48 just five years later at Hockenheim, the team suffered a severe blow, despite Graham Hill's victory in the drivers' championship.

The team is famous for developing the mid-engine layout which is popular in Indy cars and for creating the first monocoque Formula One chassis. It is also renowned for its innovation of integrating the engine and transaxle as chassis components and was among F1 pioneers of the wings and shaping of the undercarriage of the cars. This created a down-force which gave better results.

Lotus was also responsible for first moving radiators to the sides of the racing car which enabled a slicker aerodynamic performance. In addition, the company invented active suspensions for their cars and have done much to improve and sustain the performance and quality of F1 cars over the sport's long established history.

▼ Derek Warwick drives a collaboration between Lotus and Lamborghini.

Malaysia

▼ Eddie Irvine winning the first ever race at Sepang.

Held in Kuala Lumpur, at the Sepang International Circuit, the Malaysian Grand Prix is held in the first half of the season of the F1 calendar in March each year. The fastest lap time was recorded by Juan Pablo Montoya in 2004 with a time of 1:34.223 on the 5.543 kilometre circuit. The total race distance is 310.408 kilometres consisting of 56 laps. To date there have been 10 Grands Prix held at the highly-modern current course although racing formally began during the early 1960s at the Thompson Road Circuit in Singapore when the country was still part of the Malaysian federation. Singapore was eventually expelled from the federation in 1965, however, the Grand Prix continued until 1973.

The current track in Malaysia is particularly challenging for teams and drivers alike with its tropical heat, storms and complicated circuit. The Sepang

▲ A section of the pits at Sepang.

Circuit hosted its inaugural Grand Prix in 1999 and Michael Schumacher chose the event as his comeback having recovered from a broken leg suffered at Silverstone. It was eventually Eddie Irvine who would be crowned victor that day having followed his team-mate for much of the race.

Mansell

Born in Worcestershire on 8 August
1953, Nigel Ernest James Mansell, set F1
racing in the UK alight when he looked
set to win the drivers' championship in
1991. His long career in F1 spanned 15
seasons between 1980–1992 and 1994–
1995 and during this time he earned
himself a total of 480 career points, 31

wins, 59 podium appearances and 32
pole positions. He was originally an
aerospace engineer before giving it all
up to become a full-time racing driver.

Despite parental disapproval, Mansell
took up Formula Ford racing in 1976
and took the step into Formula Three
(even though he'd suffered a particularly
nasty accident at Brands Hatch) in 1978.
His form proved consistent and in 1980
he made his debut with Lotus in F1 at

the Austrian Grand Prix. He stayed with
the team for four years before moving
to Williams in 1985.

By 1988 he had been selected
by Enzo Ferrari personally (the last
driver to be picked by the great man
himself) for the start of the 1989 season.
However, he was back with Williams
for the 1991 season and his second stint
with the team was to prove even better
than his first. Mansell had his best season
ever in 1992, winning the championship.
He retired from F1 racing in favour of
the CART IndyCar World Series.

◄ Nigel Mansell
holds the trophy
aloft after winning
at Imola, 1992.

▼ Nigel Mansell
sets the best time
with his Williams
Renault during
the first practice
in Monaco, May
1992.

Matra

Marcel Chassagny founded the CAPRA aeronautical engineering company before the outbreak of the Second World War and then changed the company name to Engins Mecanique Aviation-Traction (MATRA) in 1942. Following the war, Chassagny helped Rene Bonnet and Charles Deutsch build minor formula racing cars and sports cars from his premises. Over the years there were many changes to the company and its staff, but Chassagny deduced that motor sports was the avenue through which he should promote his company. He set up MATRA Sports and the first MATRA F3 car was designed in 1965 by Paul Carillo.

By the following year the team had established itself in F2. Further success followed in both F2 and F3 and MATRA became part of F1 at the end of the 1960s. In 1974 MATRA began to dominate with its sports cars and clocked up their second constructors' title following nine wins in 10 races. The first racing car consisted of a Cosworth engine which was based on an old Rene Bonnet design. The cars made their debut at Monaco with drivers Jean-Pierre Jaussaud and Eric Offenstadt.

McLaren

Born on 30 August 1937 in Auckland, New Zealand, Bruce Leslie McLaren's name still lives on in Team McLaren. The team, under the guidance of its founder, is one of the most successful in the entire history of F1 racing. McLaren was not just a driver and team owner, he was also a race car designer, an engineer and inventor. Team McLaren have won no less than 20 world championships between constructors' and drivers' titles.

Bruce McLaren's F1 championship career began in 1959 when he made his debut at the German Grand Prix. He didn't win a world title as a driver himself, but he did take part in 104 races (he won on four occasions) and found himself on the podium 27 times. Sadly, McLaren died after a long and successful career (in all aspects of Team McLaren) while testing his new M8D at Goodwood on 2 June 1970. Despite its huge loss, the team continued to develop and prosper under the guidance of team principal Ron Dennis who was recruited in 1980. For the 2008 season, Lewis Hamilton and Heikki Kovalainen were the drivers carrying the flag.

Monaco

With its 78 laps of 3.340 kilometres, the Circuit de Monaco is a popular and challenging course for drivers and teams alike. The total race distance is 260.520 kilometres and most wins have been claimed here by Ayrton Senna with six.

The 2007 Grand Prix was won by Fernando Alonso for McLaren-Mercedes from pole position and this race is so exciting that it is generally considered as "The Jewel in the Formula One Crown". Alongside the Indy500 and the Le Mans 24 hours race it forms the Triple Crown of motor sport and is one of the most important and prestigious events on the F1 calendar. The first race took place at

▲ The street circuit of Monaco, looking out towards the marina.

◄ The Mercedes McLaren of Lewis Hamilton, 2008.

▲ Fernando
Alonso drives
ahead of team
mate Lewis
Hamilton at
Monaco, May
2007.

Monaco in 1929 and was won
by William Grover-Williams
behind the wheel of a Bugatti.
Monaco was also part of the first
ever Grands Prix in 1950.

The circuit itself is particularly
narrow along the streets of Monaco
and has a considerable number

of tight corners and steep climbs.
This keeps drivers' speeds down,
however, the course is so demanding
that it is considered a particularly
dangerous circuit with few overtaking
opportunities. It is one of the few
circuits to be used consistently
throughout the history of F1 racing.

Moss

The legendary Stirling Moss was born on 17 September 1929 in London and his name will be forever synonymous with Formula One motor racing. Despite the fact that Moss never claimed the world title, he is still considered to be one of the greatest drivers of all time. He raced a total of 66 times and clocked up 185 career points and 16 wins with 24 podium finishes. His career was particularly prolific between 1948 and 1962 and, as was common at the time, he participated

▼ Stirling Moss during the 1954 Italian Grand Prix at Monza.

▲ Stirling Moss in action during the Silverstone Grand Prix in 1956.

▶ A rather dirty Stirling Moss after winning the 1955 British Grand Prix at Aintree.

in 1990, received the 2005 Segrave Trophy and was awarded the FIA gold medal in recognition of his outstanding contribution to motor sports in 2006.

in a number of different types of race. In fact, during his racing years, Moss competed in more than 497 races.

Moss became a pioneer of British Formula One racing and made his debut at the 1951 Swiss Grand Prix. His first win came in 1955 at Silverstone while his last victory was six years later at the 1961 event in Germany. His final F1 race came in the US that same season. After retiring from the sport, Moss was honoured a number of times and was inducted into the International Motorsports Hall of Fame

Nannini

In 1990 a helicopter crash left Nannini with a severed arm and, although his forearm was repaired through surgery, his F1 career was effectively over. He began a successful career in Touring despite only partial use of his right hand and demonstrated the potential he might have had if his career hadn't been cut so tragically short.

O ften referred to as Sandro, Alessandro Nannini was born in Siena, Italy, on 7 July 1959. Active in F1 between 1986 and 1990, Nannini made his debut at the Brazilian Grand Prix and achieved one win from his 76 starts in 78 races. He clocked up 65 championship points in his fairly short career and claimed nine podium finishes. He moved to Benetton from Minardi in 1988 and immediately set out to impress. He qualified in fourth for his second race with the team and finished third in the British Grand Prix at Silverstone. Nannini went on to take the lead at the Japanese Grand Prix after the two leaders, Senna and Prost, collided. When Senna rejoined the race, Nannini lost his first position. However, the Brazilian was disqualified and it gave the Italian his one and only win in Formula One.

◀ Alessandro Nannini in action in his Minardi MM during the 1986 Brazilian Grand Prix.

Oliver

▼ Jackie Oliver in a 1970 BRM F 153 at Brands Hatch.

Keith Jack "Jackie" Oliver made his Grand Prix debut at the 1967 German race. Born in Essex on

14 August 1942, his F1 career was fairly short-lived. Today he is perhaps better known as the founder of the Arrows team than as a racing driver.

His career began in 1961 in a Mini in British Club Saloon racing but he soon moved into GT racing and Formula Three where he showed his ability for speed. However, his car was blighted by mechanical problems and he joined Team Lotus in F2 for the 1967 season. It was the tragic death of Jim Clark that saw Oliver called up for F1. Colin Chapman hired him for the team in F1 in 1968 but he moved to BRM the following year.

Disappointingly, the move would end his F1 career with constant BRM breakdowns and other mechanical faults. In 1973 when Shadow entered F1, Oliver was nominated as team leader. In 1977 he formed the Arrows Grand Prix team and ultimately became famous when the newly formed side suffered the longest losing streak in F1 history. They competed in 382 races with no wins.

Piquet

The Brazilian driver was a three-time world champion in 1981, 1983 and 1987. Born, Nelson Piquet Souto Maior – better known by his first two names – on 17 August 1952, he began kart racing at the age of 14. His politician father disapproved of his son racing so Piquet used his mother's maiden name, to hide his identity. He quickly moved up through the ranks and arrived in Europe hailed as a prodigy. He moved into F1 in 1978 and made his debut at the German Grand Prix that same year.

He was a consistent challenger for the championship with the Brabham team and was first to claim the title with a turbo engine in 1983 before moving to Williams in 1986 to partner his long-time rival Nigel Mansell. Piquet won the championship again in 1987 and moved to Lotus the following season. His form suffered and he became regarded as a loose cannon with his outspoken remarks. However, he regained his previous form in the early 1990s. His son, Nelson Angelo Piquet, has followed in his father's footsteps and became a Formula One star during 2008 with the Renault team alongside Alonso.

▲ Nelson Piquet in his Braham-Alfa Romeo during the 1979 Grand Prix season.

Prost

▶ Alain Prost
holds the trophy
aloft after his
victory in the
Brazilian Grand
Prix, 1988.

▼ Alain Prost on a
lap of honour after
winning the world
championship in
1993.

Born on 24 February 1955 in France, Alain Marie Pascal Prost claimed four championships between 1985 and 1993. His debut in F1 came in the Argentine Grand Prix in 1980 and he went on to form intense rivalries with Ayrton Senna and Nigel Mansell. His first win was at his native Grand Prix in France in 1981. He won the championship two years running in 1985 and 1986 but was unable to claim a hat-trick of titles

in 1987. It was Senna's collision with Prost at the Japanese Grand Prix in 1989 that gave the talented driver his third championship.

A year later, with Prost now driving for Ferrari, they collided again, but Prost, this time, didn't pick up the title. After taking a year out in 1992, Prost was once again behind the wheel in 1993. He suffered a controversial time while at Ferrari, but joined Williams on his return. The car was competitive, Prost had the right attitude and the 1993 championship was his. However, he retired from F1 racing at the end of the season when Senna signed for Williams for 1994.

Quester

Austrian Dieter Quester had an extremely short-lived career in Formula One. He had one start out of two races and his debut was abruptly halted at the German Grand Prix in 1969. Born in Vienna on 30 May 1939, Quester began his racing career in motorboats during the 1950s then went on to become part of the Formula Two team with BMW. His debut was somewhat overshadowed by the death of his team-mate, Gerhard Mitter, who died practising at Nurburgring in the BMW 269. As a suspension or steering failure was blamed for the crash it was decided that Quester should withdraw from the race. Hubert Hahne and Hans Herrmann of Porsche also pulled out of the Grand Prix.

Quester's debut came the following year at the Austrian Grand Prix on 18 August 1974. Despite an impressive first outing (he finished a respectable ninth), Quester decided to concentrate on the European Touring Car Championship and he has competed in more than 50 24 hour races. Quester remained active in Touring and, in January 2006, he won the 24 hour race at Dubai Autodrome with Hans-Joachim Stuck, Philipp Peter and Toto Wolff. He repeated the win in 2007 and in September that year, he won the 24 hour race at Silverstone.

▼ Quester now takes part in touring car championships.

Raikkonen

▶ Kimi Raikkonen celebrates after winning the race and the F1 world championship at the Brazilian Grand Prix, October 2007.

The reigning world champion going into the 2008 season was Kimi Raikkonen from Finland. Born on 17 October 1979, he began his Formula One career with Sauber-Petronas in 2001 as a regular driver and moved

to McLaren–Mercedes a year later where his potential was plain to see; he finished as runner up in the 2003 and 2005 campaigns behind Michael Schumacher and Fernando Alonso respectively. He joined Ferrari for the start of the 2007 season and became the highest paid driver in the history of F1.

Raikkonen's 2007 championship was secured by just one point over rookie Lewis Hamilton and the more experienced Fernando Alonso. However, the young driver from Finland had

already gleaned himself the nickname "Iceman" for his calm, cool and calculated style of driving. Although to the team mechanics he's known as Kimppa, Raikka or Kimster.

Raikkonen began in karting at the age of 10. His potential was so enormous that Peter Sauber gave the Finn a test with Sauber F1 in September 2000 and persuaded the FIA to grant Raikkonen his Super Licence on the strength of his potential performance. Sauber was right to put his faith in Raikkonen as the Finn looks set to dominate the racing fraternity for some time to come.

▲ Kimi Raikkonen in his 2008 Ferrari.

◄ Driving for Sauber in 2001.

Red Bull

Red Bull Racing was founded in 2005 and is today based in Milton Keynes in the UK. This newly formed team hasn't yet had time to clock up any major victories or championship wins, however, that doesn't stop the company from being serious about winning races. That was proved by the team's move to secure the services of Adrian Newey as technical director in 2006.

The 2007 season saw Red Bull using a Newey-designed car for the first time. They were aiming for at least fifth place in the constructors' championship at the close of the campaign. Another important decision that came about for the season was the introduction of the championship-winning Renault engine in place of the Ferrari engine that had been incorporated in the cars from the team's formation. The team's drivers, David Coulthard and Mark Webber, were expected to bring strength and experience to the mix.

Red Bull is run by former driver Christian Horner who, approaching his mid-30s, is the youngest team director in F1. The origins of Red Bull began as Stewart Grand Prix in 1997 and was later taken over by Ford who changed the team name to Jaguar. The mix was not a success but Red Bull is set to change all that.

THE A TO Z OF GRAND PRIX

Flavio Briatore of Renault carries the constructors' and champion's trophies after Fernando Alonso won the Monaco Grand Prix, May 2006.

Renault

From the late 1970s, Renault F1 has been competing in motor sports both as a constructor and engine supplier. The team is based in Enstone, Oxfordshire, although the engines themselves are manufactured in France. Renault F1 has had both success at constructor and driver levels and claimed their first victory in 1992. Further success followed – particularly when supplying engines to Williams – in the drivers' world championship in 1993, 1995, 1996 and again in 1997. Contructors' titles came in 1992, 1993, 1994, 1995, 1996 and 1997. Having had such a prolific decade it was no surprise when further success was Renault's in 2005

 RENAULT

and 2006.

As a highly competent outfit the team pulled out of Formula One at the end of the 1997 season, in part, because of the departure of designer and team principal Adrian Newey. However, they were back by March 2000 when Renault purchased Benetton Formula One. They kept the Benetton name for two seasons but rebranded themselves as Renault F1 in 2002. Fernando Alonso claimed the drivers' title in 2005 and 2006 before rejoining the team for the 2008 season with newly promoted test driver Nelson Angelo Piquet.

▲ Fernando Alonso's Renault at the Singapore Grand Prix, 2008.

▶ Giancarlo Fisichella's Renault.

Rindt

Karl Jochen Rindt became the only
Formula One world champion to be
awarded the honour posthumously.
Born in Mainz, Germany, on 18
April 1942, Rindt was brought up in
Austria by his grandparents following
his parents' deaths from a bombing
raid during the Second World War.
It was here that he began his racing
career where his potential shone in
Formula Two. His F1 debut came at the
1964 Austrian Grand Prix, however,
his first season was short-lived.

His early career was blighted by cars
that didn't match his fast driving speed
and versatility and it wasn't until 1969
that his full potential was realised. His
1970 season was exceptional and he was
well on his way to making the drivers'
world championship his own with wins
in the US, Monaco, the Netherlands,
France, the UK and Germany. While
practising for the Italian Grand Prix he
was tragically killed, however, his strong
lead in the championship was enough
to secure him the title. He had already
suggested that he would retire from F1
if he won the 1970 championship which
given the circumstances was sadly ironic.

▲ Jochen Rindt at
the 1966 French
Grand Prix.

Rosberg

Born in Solna, Stockholm in Sweden on 6 December 1948, Keijo "Keke" Rosberg had a relatively late start to his F1 career. His debut came at the 1978 South African Grand Prix when Rosberg was already 29 years old. He'd enjoyed a fairly prolific time in Formula Vee and Formula Atlantic followed by a successful career in Formula Two before coming to prominence in F1. He was an integral member of the Wolf team, who were experiencing financial difficulties by the second half of the 1979 season, and Rosberg signed for Fittipaldi Automotive. However, his form during 1980 wasn't spectacular and in 1981 he failed to score at all. All that was about to change with the advent of Williams.

The Williams team were interested in the Swede despite his current lack of form and the mix proved to be a magical formula. With a competitive car, Rosberg was able to focus on the challenge and he was rewarded with his first, and only, championship at the end of the 1982 season. His last win came at the Australian Grand Prix in 1985 and he retired from Formula One after the same race the following year.

Scheckter

South African Jody David Scheckter was born on 29 January 1950 and claimed his only drivers' championship in 1979 at what was basically the end of his F1 career. He had come to the sport seven years earlier when he made his Grand Prix debut in the United States in 1972 with McLaren. His third place at his first race seemed assured until an unfortunate spin saw him finish in ninth place. Scheckter's first season also saw the South African – who moved to the UK in 1970 – score eight points in consecutive races and he finished overall in third place in the championship.

The following season wasn't quite as spectacular for Scheckter, however, his third year in the sport saw him, again, come third overall. He was the last driver to win a championship for Ferrari in 1979, until Michael Schumacher proved his worth some 21 years later.

His last win in F1 came in 1979 at the Italian Grand Prix while his last race was akin to his debut at Watkins Glen in the US. Today, Scheckter is an organic farmer in the Home Counties.

Schumacher

▲ Michael
Schumacher in
his Jordan at his
debut F1 race in
Belgium in 1991.

Seven-time world champion Michael
Schumacher began his career in karting
at the age of 12 and eventually went
on to break all records and become the
most successful F1 driver of all time.
Born on 3 January 1969 in Germany,
the young Schumacher, by law, was
required to wait for his license until
the age of 14, however, having won

his first club championship at the age
of six, he travelled to Luxembourg
to gain the required paperwork.
His Formula One debut came at
the Belgian Grand Prix in 1991.

Schumacher was already renowned
for his abilities and exceptional speed.
He was confident of producing fast
laps at the crucial moment in a race
and was skilled enough to push his
car to the very limit for a sustained
period of time. It was just the winning

formula that the sport required and, to many, Schumacher is the greatest driver of all time. His first championship was won in 1994 with Benetton.

He defended his title the following year and then waited five years to claim his third overall victory, this time with Ferrari. His fourth championship win came in 2001 and he successfully beat all other rivals to dominate motor sports' top prize from 2002 to 2004. He announced his retirement from F1 after appearing on the podium at the Italian Grand Prix in 2006. His younger brother, Ralf, is an accomplished driver in F1 but failed to match his brother's success before retiring at the end of the 2007 season when he failed to secure a drive.

▲ A pensive Michael Schumacher adjusting his helmet.

◄ Michael Schumacher at the Brazilian Grand Prix, the last race of his career.

Senna

▶ Ayrton Senna in his Lotus at the Belgian Grand Prix, 1986.

▼ Ayrton Senna in action during the Monaco Grand Prix, June 1984.

Born on 21 March 1960, Brazilian Ayrton Senna da Silva died doing what he loved best — racing. The three-times championship winner made his debut in his native Brazil in 1984 having been a kart racer from an early age. He started with Toleman where he soon discovered that he would have a heated rivalry with Frenchman Alain Prost. The two drivers' on-track (and off in some instances) clashes became legendary throughout the 1980s and early 1990s. However, despite being renowned for his fearsome quality and determination to win on the circuit, Senna was also revered for his compassion and humanitarian attitude when not racing.

In similar fashion to a young German who would come to idolise him (Michael Schumacher), Senna had the tendency to push the barriers of fairness while racing to the limit and was often at the centre of controversy. Also, like Schumacher, Senna would push his car to the limit and would often go flat out. His last team, following his stints with Lotus and a successful run with McLaren, was Williams. Senna's death on 1 May 1994, at Imola on the San Marino Grand Prix, shocked the world. He entered the Tamburello corner at high speed, however, his car left the track and he crashed into a concrete wall at around 135 miles per hour. It was found that the suspension of the detached front wheel had pierced his helmet.

Singapore

Having been absent from F1 for a number of years, the first Grand Prix to again take place in Singapore was on 28 September 2008 on a street circuit which was given FIA approval in 2007. This historic event proved to be a first in the sport's history as the race was contested after the sun had set. To prepare for this immense change, the drivers were required to practice and qualify at night in order to get used to driving in the dark. The first race in Singapore was held in 1961 but renamed the Malaysian Grand Prix in 1962.

When Singapore gained its independence in 1965, the race was once again named appropriately. But, the event was abandoned after the 1973 season for a number of reasons including fatalities. The length of the laps on the current street circuit are 5.067 kilometres located in the Marina

Bay area where powerful lighting was installed to replicate daylight conditions. With 61 laps of technically challenging corners, the 2008 Singapore Grand Prix provided an exciting spectacle for the 80,000 spectators with pit lane incidents and the deployment of the safety car having a dramatic effect on the outcome of the race that saw Fernando Alonso claim his 20th victory after starting 15th on the grid.

▼ Spectators watch as the cars speed past the grand stand at the Singapore Grand Prix, September 2008.

Spain

▲ Spanish
fans supporting
their local hero
Fernando Alonso
at the Circuit de
Catalunya, 2008 .

▶ The finishing
line at the Circuit
de Catalunya.

The race length of the Circuit de Catalunya in Spain is 302.449 kilometres consisting of 65 laps with a distance of 4.655 kilometres. The first Spanish race ran to touring car rules in 1913 and was called a Grand Prix. Races had, however, been taking place in the country since 1908 (the Catalan Cup). The purpose-built track at Sitges, near Barcelona, fell into financial difficulties and the Circuito Lasarte became the preferred venue. However, when civil war broke out in Spain in 1936 racing was abandoned. International racing wasn't reintroduced until 1951.

The Pedralbes Circuit became Spain's Formula One championship venue, but a horrific accident at Le Man in 1955

brought spectator safety into question and the circuit was dropped from the F1 calendar. After a successful comeback in the early 1960s, the Spanish Grand Prix was once again hampered by a tragic accident at the 1975 event. Four spectators were killed when the rear wing of Rolf Stommelen's car broke off. The race was then confined to Jarama, north of Madrid, before other venues were introduced. The current track near Barcelona was finished for the 1991 Grand Prix where it has remained ever since.

Stewart

Sir John Young Stewart, better known as Jackie, was born in Milton, West Dunbartonshire on 11 June 1939. The three-times world champion (1969, 1971, 1973), was nicknamed "The Flying Scot" and was active in Formula One between 1965 and 1973. His career began in F3 for Tyrrell and he made his debut with F1 at the South African Grand Prix in 1965 which started a run of 109 races with 99 starts, 27 wins, 43 podium finishes and a respectable 359 career points. Stewart's first win in Formula One came at the Italian Grand Prix in his debut season. His final win took place at the 1973 German event and he retired from driving following the US Grand Prix that same year.

Having finished his driving career, Stewart became a team owner with his son Paul when they set up Stewart Grand Prix Formula One racing between 1997 and 1999. A constant

▲ Jackie Stewart with a clear lead in the 1966 Monaco Grand Prix.

▲ Jackie Stewart in the pits at Silverstone with his Matra Ford during the first qualifying session for the British Grand Prix, 1969.

presence in Formula One, Stewart is a popular racing commentator in the United States. After crashing out of the Spa Grand Prix in 1966 (where he could well have died) Stewart became an advocate for racing safety. During his own driving career the chances of a fatal crash were two out of three and he campaigned with BRM team boss Louis Stanley for well equipped emergency services and more effective (and safer) barriers around race tracks.

Super Aguri

The Super Aguri F1 team made their debut in the 2006 season, founded by Aguri Suzuki, a former F1 driver. The team is based in Tokyo, Japan, with operations in the UK. Using the Honda RA807E 2.4 V8 engine, the team cars are known as Super Aguri Hondas. The team's first two drivers were Takuma Sato and Yuji Ide, supported by Frank Montagny, but after just four races, the third driver replaced Ide in the second driver role before the European Grand Prix. Super Aguri made their debut at the Bahrain Grand Prix in 2006 and competed in 39 races before encountering financial difficulties in May 2008, withdrawing from F1.

Despite being a relative newcomer to F1, the team secured a ninth place finish overall in the 2007 championship with four points. For the 2008 season, it was announced that Super Aguri would be retaining the services of Takuma Sato and Anthony Davidson. Although the drivers appeared on the FIA's list for the season, Super Aguri were still in negotiations with their sponsors and at the start of the season contracts were without signatures. The Spanish Grand Prix was the race that the team decided to introduce their SA08 to F1 racing.

▲ Super Aguri at their debut at the Bahrain Grand Prix.

▼ Takuma Sato of Japan and team Super Aguri F1 testing at the Circuit de Catalunya in 2006.

Surtees

John Surtees was born on 11 February 1934 and was a renowned Grand Prix

motorcyclist and Formula One racing driver from Surrey. His motorcycle career began some eight years before he made his debut in F1 at the 1960 Monaco Grand Prix. For 12 years, Surtees was a prolific driver and claimed his first championship win at the German Grand Prix in 1963. However, it was nearly all over for Surtees the year following his triumphant championship title in 1964. He suffered a horrific accident at the Mosport Circuit in Ontario, Canada in September 1965 while practising, but after recovering, he was back to F1 for the start of the 1966 season. Surtees took his last win at the Italian Grand Prix in 1967 and retired from the sport after the 1972 event, again, in Italy.

Two years prior to retiring as a driver, Surtees formed his own race team, the Surtees Racing Organisation, and went on to spend nine seasons in Formula One, Formula Two and Formula 5000. He is a seven-times winner of the Grand Prix motorcycle title on both 350cc and 500cc bikes and was inducted into the International Motorsports Hall of Fame in 1996.

Toro

Scuderia Toro Rosso, Italian for Red Bull Stable, made its team debut at the 2006 Bahrain Grand Prix. The racing team was formed by former Formula One driver Gerhard Berger and drinks company Red Bull. It is the sister team of Red Bull Racing and for the 2007 and 2008 seasons used Ferrari V8 engines. Today's team principal is Franz Tost while the team's car was designed by the renowned Adrian Newey. For 2008 the team drivers comprised Sebastian Vettel (formerly of BMW–Sauber) and Sebastien Bourdais.

Under the supervision of technical director Giorgio Ascanelli, the company is based in Faenza, Italy and has competed in more than 50 races since its debut. The 2007 season proved disappointing for the team where poor reliability and driver errors were blamed for a lack of form. The team suffered a

particularly low finishing record. As a result, Scott Speed was dropped from the team and Vettel took his place. Red Bull originally bought out Paul Stoddart's Minardi which was one of the least competitive teams in F1. Under contractual obligations, the team must remain based in Italy for the time being. Red Bull did drop the Minardi name much to the fans' disappointment.

▲ Success for Toro Rosso at the 2008 Italian Grand Prix.

◀ John Surtees in his Ferrari during the Syracuse Grand Prix, 1966.

Toyota

▲ Timo Glock in his Toyota driving at speed at the Italian Grand Prix, 2008.

▶ Jarno Trulli, one of Toyota's drivers.

Panasonic Toyota Racing, usually referred to as Toyota F1, was formed in 1999 and announced plans to participate in Formula One. Based in Cologne, Germany, the team is headed by team principal Tadashi Yamashina while team drivers include Jarno Trulli and Timo Glock. The team made their debut at the 2002 Australian Grand Prix and since inception have competed in just over 120 F1 events. However, to date, the team have yet to claim any major championships. They finished the 2007 season in sixth place with a total of 13 points.

Ralf Schumacher was a notable driver for Toyota, joining the team in 2005 from Williams. He left the team more than two years later in October for new challenges; although he didn't state what these might be. Schumacher achieved the team's fastest lap time when he competed in the 2005 Belgian Grand Prix. Jarno Trulli was snapped up by Toyota for the start of the 2005 season and settled well with the team. As one of the few teams in F1 never to have sponsorship from a large tobacco manufacturer, Toyota have worked closely with the likes of Panasonic, Kingfisher Airlines, Denso and Esso.

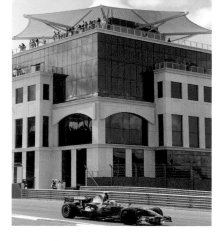

Turkey

The first Grand Prix in Turkey took place on 21 August 2005 at the purpose-built Istanbul Park Circuit. It was constructed by German civil engineer Hermann Tilke and is one of three anti-clockwise circuits on the Formula One calendar; the other two being located in Italy and Brazil. The total race length at Istanbul is 309.72 kilometres made up of 57 laps of 5.34 kilometres.

On three of the four occasions that the track has been used, Ferrari have won on the circuit that closely follows the contours of the land. The circuit dips and falls and Turn 8 is considered one of the best on the track; the quadruple apex corner is four corners joined

together and it is extremely challenging for the drivers. As a marvellous feat in engineering, the circuit takes its influences from world renowned courses, particularly Autodromo Jose Carlos Pace in Brazil and the Spa-Francorchamps. At the first Grand Prix in 2005, the circuit became famous for the number of drivers spinning off the track. At the 2008 Grand Prix, Felipe Massa won the race in one hour, 26 minutes and 49.451 seconds.

◀ Felipe Massa on his way to his third victory at the Turkish Grand Prix, 2008.

▼ The circuit under construction just outside Istanbul.

Tyrrell

Founded by Ken Tyrrell in 1958, the
Tyrrell Racing Organisation started
building its own cars for Formula One
in 1970. The early part of that decade
reaped huge successes for the team
who went on to win three drivers'
championships and one constructors'
title (1971). Ken Tyrrell began racing
in Formula Three but, quickly
realising that he had more potential
as a constructor than a driver, stood
down in 1959.

Tyrrell started out as a Formula
Junior operation and worked through
the lower Formulas giving races to
John Surtees and Jacky Ickx in the
early 1960s. It was the arrival of
Jackie Stewart in 1963 that really
set the team on fire and in the mid
to late-1960s Tyrrell was prolific in
Formula Two. Elf and Ford both
helped Tyrrell realise its dream in
Formula One.

Jackie Stewart, meanwhile,
became a serious contender for
the championship in a Tyrrell-run
Matra MS10 with its innovative
aviation-inspired structural fuel tanks.
Unfortunately, the car was considered
unsafe by the FIA and was banned for
the 1970 season. The team's debut had
come at the 1968 South African Grand
Prix and its first drivers' championship
was won the following year. The team
astounded the racing fraternity when it
unveiled its six-wheeled P34 in 1976, a
car that had limited success.

Unser

Robert "Bobby" William Unser was born on 20 February 1934 in Colorado, United States and was one of seven drivers to win the Indianapolis 500 on no less than three occasions. He is also one of only two drivers to have won the event in three different decades including the 1960s, 1970s and 1980s. Hailing from Colorado Springs, the American is brother of Al Unser and Jerry Unser. He is also the father of Robby Unser.

He was more renowned for his 500 races than he was for his short-lived Formula One career, however, under the Owen Racing Organisation he made his debut in the sport in 1968 driving a BRM V12. Although he only competed in two Grands Prix, Unser's Indy 500 results were more than impressive and showed why he had been given a drive.

At his debut in 1963 he finished in 33rd place after crashing on the second lap. He bettered this result the following year and by 1966 had managed to secure himself sixth place overall. In 1968 he took his first win, a feat he would repeat in 1972 and 1975 as well as again in 1981. However, his finish in 1981 was one of the most controversial in Indy 500 history. In lap 49, Unser and Andretti headed back to the race following a pit stop during a caution period and Unser passed eight cars.

▼ Bobby Unser at the Indianapolis 500.

Villeneuve

V

S on of the famous Gilles Villeneuve,
Jacques Joseph Charles Villeneuve
was born on 9 April 1971 in Quebec,
Canada. He had two extremely
successful years in CART before joining
Formula One where he challenged
Damon Hill for the championship
title in his debut year. His first F1 race

▶ Jacques
Villeneuve takes
the chequered flag
in his Williams-
Renault to win the
Hungarian Grand
Prix, 1997.

came at the 1996 Australian Grand Prix at the start of the season and, during his rookie year, he won his first race at the European Grand Prix.

It must have been exhilarating for the young Canadian who followed in his father's footsteps despite his fatal accident while practising for the Belgian Grand Prix in 1982. He asked his mother if he could become a racing driver and she agreed on the condition that he worked hard to gain good marks in his maths (one of his weakest subjects). Villeneuve applied himself, gained the marks he needed and his mother, Joann, fulfilled her promise.

His first F1 win came at the 1996 European Grand Prix while his last was the 1997 Luxembourg event, the same year he claimed the world title. He retired from Formula One following a lack of form after the 2006 German Grand Prix and took up racing for Peugeot in the 24 hours Le Mans and NASCAR in 2007. He has also released the album *Private Paradise* since giving up F1.

▲ Villeneuve and the Williams Renault team on his way to third place during the German Grand Prix at Hockenheimring, Germany, 1996.

Williams

Williams Grand Prix Engineering Ltd, more commonly known as Williams F1, made their debut in the sport at the 1978 Argentine Grand Prix. As one of the most high-profile constructors, Williams F1 has enjoyed a long and established reputation within Formula One. Formed by Sir Frank Williams and Patrick Head in 1977, the team celebrated its first drivers' victory at the 1979 Grand Prix at Silverstone with Clay Regazzoni, from Switzerland, behind the wheel.

Jacques Villeneuve would win the team's 100th race in 1997 and this ranked Williams alongside Ferrari and McLaren who had also achieved 100 wins in F1. The team have employed a number of highly-successful drivers including Keke Rosberg, Alain Prost, Ayrton Senna, Nelson Piquet,

Damon Hill and Nigel Mansell.

Senna's death in 1994 caused some controversy for the team who were investigated. In fact, Williams, Head and designer Adrian Newey were all accused of manslaughter. All three were cleared of the charges and the trial finally came to an end leaving the team to once again focus on their racing results. Between 1980 and 1997, Williams F1 held the title of most constructors' championships (this was overtaken by Ferrari in 2000). The team have competed in more than 515 races and have had seven victories in the drivers' championship.

▲ The 2008 car for Williams.

Xtreme Moments

▲ Roland
Ratzenberger
just after the
spectacular
crash that cost
him his life.

S adly, many drivers have died in
Formula One pursuing the ultimate
goal of the world championship.
Some met their untimely end during
practice sessions, others while driving
in races. However, some of the
most extreme moments have been

mentioned elsewhere in this book.

The most fatal accidents have occured at the Nurburgring, in Germany. There have been five fatalities at the Grand Prix circuit. Modena Autodrome and Autodromo Nazionale Monza have each witnessed three fatal crashes. Five circuits, including Silverstone, have been the site of two fatal accidents, while 11 Grand Prix circuits including Italy (Reims) and Rouen-Les-Essarts in France have had one fatality.

◀ Stuart Lewis-Evans a month before his fatal crash.

◀◀ Francois Cevert who died at the esses at Watkins Glen in 1973.

- *Chet Miller, United States, 15 May 1953*
- *Carl Scarborough, United States, 30 May 1953*
- *Eugenio Castellotti, Italy, 14 March 1957*
- *Stuart Lewis-Evans, Great Britain, 19 September 1958*
- *Chris Bristow, Great Britain, 19 June 1960*
- *Giulio Cabianca, Italy, 15 June 1961*
- *Ricardo Rodriguez, Mexico, 1 November 1962*
- *Carel Godin de Beaufort, the Netherlands, 2 August 1964*
- *Jo Schlesser, France, 7 July 1968*
- *Gerhard Mitter, Germany, 2 August 1969*
- *Piers Courage, Great Britain, 7 June 1970*
- *Francois Cevert, France, 7 October 1973*
- *Peter Revson, United States, 22 March 1974*
- *Ronnie Peterson, Sweden, 11 September 1978*
- *Patrick Depailler, France, 1 August 1980*
- *Riccardo Paletti, Italy, 13 June 1982*
- *Roland Ratzenberger, Austria, 30 April 1994*

witnessed by millions of spectators through worldwide television coverage. The list on the right is just a few of the 43 drivers across the globe who have lost their lives behind the wheel of a racing car who are not

Yamamoto

Japanese driver Sakon Yamamoto was born in the Aichi Prefecture on 9 July 1982 and made his debut in F1 at the 2006 German Grand Prix. The young driver began his career in karting at

the Suzuka Circuit School and worked his way up to become test driver (third driver) for the Jordan Formula One team – for one weekend only – at the 2005 Japanese Grand Prix. He joined

Super Aguri in June 2006 as a test driver and replaced Montagny at Hockenheim, but his career was slow to take off.

Mechanical failures and a stalled engine did little to encourage Yamamoto who managed a total of one lap during his first two races. He was consigned to last place on the grid for the Italian Grand Prix in his debut season but the car suffered hydraulic problems and he was forced to retire from the race. A milestone was reached when Yamamoto managed to finish a race for the first time in China (2006). By the end of his first season he had managed a respectable three consecutive finishes but he was replaced by Anthony Davidson for Aguri for the 2007 campaign. Yamamoto is currently on the team for ING Renault F1.

▲ Sakon Yamamoto at the Chinese Grand Prix where he finished a race for the first time.

Zanardi

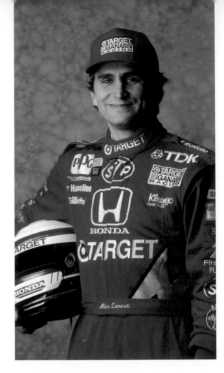

► Alessandro Zanardi in 1996.
►► Alessandro Zanardi driving for Jordan at the Japanese Grand Prix, 1991.

Alessandro "Alex" Zanardi was born in Bologna, Italy, on 23 October 1966 and won two CART championship titles in the US during the late 1990s after a fairly unsuccessful Formula One career as a driver for Jordan, Minardi, Lotus and Williams. He failed to score any notable career points in F1 (except for one point at the Brazilian Grand Prix) and never managed a championship win.

Zanardi's debut came at the Spanish Grand Prix in 1991 having enjoyed a successful start in karting and the Italian Formula Three series. He then moved into Formula 3000 with the Il Barone Rampante team and a strong campaign saw him gain the interest of Jordan. His first full season in F1 was uneventful and during 1992 he was a guest driver for Minardi for the injured Fittipaldi. After testing for

Benetton, he finally signed for Lotus for the start of the 1993 season.

He turned to Sports Car racing in 1995 when Lotus collapsed at the end of that year and in 1996 took up CART racing where he has gleaned much more success. He was back in Formula One in 1999 when Frank Williams noticed his championship-style in CART racing. However, he was dropped at the end of the year having failed to find his form.

Other books also available:

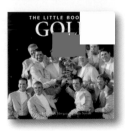

Available from all major stockists

Green**Umbrella**
Publishing

LITTLE BOOK OF THE
OLYMPICS
AN OLYMPIC A to Z
Written by Jon Stroud

THE LITTLE BOOK OF
HORSERACING
A HORSERACING A to Z

The Little Book of
CRICKET
LEGENDS

The Little Book of
GOLF
LEGENDS

The Little Book of
FOOTBALL
LEGENDS

The Little Book of
RUGBY
LEGENDS

The Little Book of
GRAND PRIX
LEGENDS

THE LITTLE BOOK OF
EUROPEAN
FOOTBALL

THE LITTLE BOOK OF
FISHING
A FISHING A to Z

THE LITTLE BOOK OF
JANE
AUSTEN

LITTLE BOOK OF THE
BRONTË
SISTERS

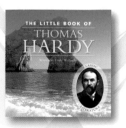

THE LITTLE BOOK OF
THOMAS
HARDY

Available from all major stockists

The pictures in this book were provided courtesy of the following:

GETTY IMAGES
101 Bayham Street, London NW1 0AG

Creative Director: Kevin Gardner

Design and Artwork: David Wildish

Picture research: Ellie Charleston

Published by Green Umbrella Publishing

Publishers Jules Gammond and Vanessa Gardner

Written by Charlotte Morgan